T0040960

BOOK OF INTERMEDIATE HORN SOLOS

Edited by **David Ohanian**
of The Canadian Brass

CONTENTS

In progressive order of difficulty, from a generally intermediate to an advanced level.

The instrument pictured on the cover is a CB40 French Horn from The Canadian Brass Collection, a line of professional brass instruments marketed by The Canadian Brass.
Photo: Gordon Janowiak

ISBN 0-7935-4542-0

7777 W. BLUEMOUND RD. P.O. BOX 13819 MILWAUKEE, WI 53213

ABOUT THE MUSIC...

Robert Schumann: Bitterness (Ich grolle nicht)

Schumann (1810-1856) was a central German figure of the Romantic movement in the arts in the nineteenth century. In his day he was an important musical critic and author, as well as being a composer of symphonies, chamber music, piano music, and art songs. He spent his adult life in Bonn, Leipzig and Dresden, and was married to one of the first famous women pianists, Clara Wieck. "Bitterness" is a transcription of one of his most celebrated songs for voice and piano, excerpted from his song cycle *Dichterliebe*, composed in 1840. Originally entitled "Ich grolle nicht" (I bear no grudge), the song is a lover's ironic and stinging response to being rejected.

Gaetano Donizetti: Lover's Lament (Una furtiva lagrima)
from *The Elixir of Love*

Donizetti (1797-1848) was one the principal popular composers of Italian opera in his day, and in the span of less than thirty years wrote nearly seventy complete operas (more than anyone else in history), besides hundreds of other compositions. Historians have also discovered many thousands of letters written by Donizetti, and between his composing and letter writing, one wonders how he ever had time for anything else! (The poor man literally drove himself crazy, and died mentally deranged.) *The Elixir of Love* is one of his most performed operas, particularly being a favorite of star tenors such as Luciano Pavarotti, who is world-famous for this opera. This very famous aria ("Una furtiva lagrima," called "Lover's Lament" here) comes near the end of the story. The peasant Nemorino is in love with a woman he thinks he will never have, and he sings this plaintive song about his feelings. (By the way, he gets the girl in the end.) (Pronunciations: Gaetano=gah -eh-TAH-no, Donizetti= do-nee-TSEHT-tee)

Hugo Wolf: The Gardener (Der Gärtner)

The Austrian Hugo Wolf (1860-1903) is the only major composer in history to concentrate almost exclusively on writing art songs for voice and piano, setting German poetry of previous eras and of his own day. Unlike the other major song composers (Schubert, Schumann, Brahms, Strauss), Wolf did not spend his career also writing symphonies, chamber music, concertos, piano music or operas, even though he was obsessed his entire life with writing a great opera and winning eternal acclaim from it. (He did compose one opera, but it was never produced during his lifetime.) Wolf was moody and eccentric, rarely had any money of his own, and was usually supported by generous friends. He battled with insanity toward the end of his life, and spent his last years in a mental institution, dying at the age of 43, largely the result of syphilis that was contracted in his youth. "The Gardener" is a song about, well... a gardener, and has a folksong quality about it. (Pronunciation tip: Wolf is pronounced voolf)

Johann Sebastian Bach: Be Thou With Me (Bist du bei mir)

When you consider the concept of lasting fame, of worldwide recognition over hundreds of years, it would be difficult to find a more permanently famous name than Bach (1685-1750). Even 250 years after his death, his music is still played and heard every day of every year by millions of people in every country of the world. He could never have guessed such an audience would be possible. During his lifetime he was more famous in Germany for his expert organ playing than for his compositions, and spent his entire life as a hardworking church musician, composing elaborate new music for nearly every Sunday, in addition to thousands of instrumental compositions and songs to be performed away from church in concerts. This lovely song "Bist du bei mir" (often sung at weddings) is one of his best-known pieces.

Gilbert and Sullivan: Welcome Joy! Adieu to Sadness from *The Sorcerer*

The great English operetta creators, Gilbert and Sullivan, were the Rodgers and Hammerstein of their day, creating the equivalent of Broadway musical comedies for London of the 1880s and 1890s. Arthur Sullivan wrote the music and W. S. Gilbert wrote the witty and politically satirical words. Their shows are still very popular, although *The Sorcerer*, one of the earlier collaborations, doesn't enjoy the fame of *H.M.S. Pinafore, The Mikado*, or *Pirates of Penzance*. It's interesting that though celebrated and successful in their collaboration, Sullivan and Gilbert never particularly liked one another, and had public battles on more than one occasion.

Wolfgang Amadeus Mozart: Cherubino's Aria from *The Marriage of Figaro*

Cheubino is an amorous teenage page in the court of Count Almaviva in this 18th century comedy classic. Cherubino is the kind of adolescent whose hormones are so sexually charged up that he wants to make love to every woman he sees, and that's what this aria is about, in fact. (And you thought classical music was stuffy!) Mozart wrote the opera in 1786, premiered it in Vienna (where he lived), saw it largely ignored, then was delighted to find that a production a few months later became a wild success in Prague. Even before his death in 1791 the opera had begun to become popular all over Europe, and has survived to be one of the five most performed operas in the world. (Pronunciation tip: Cherubino=keh-roo-BEE-no)

Friedrich von Flotow: Serenade (M'appari tutt'amor) from *Martha*

Friedrich von Flotow (1812-1883) is one of those composers who seem to be known for only one work, and in his case that is his opera *Martha*, composed in 1847. But to be even more specific, there is one tune from this one opera that's really Flotow's only hit, and that is this "Serenade." It's a wonder that a German composer could write something that sounds so quintessentially Italian! (In the 1979 hit movie "Breaking Away" the tune is played to conjure up the very soul of Italy.) If Flotow is only known today for this one melody, it certainly wasn't for lack of trying. He composed several dozen operas, symphonies, vocal pieces, etc., all of which are forgotten. Posterity *is* cruel, isn't it?

Richard Strauss: Dedication (Zueignung)

Richard Strauss (not Johann Strauss, the waltz king, by the way) must have loved the sound of the French horn, because he wrote so many heroic, exciting horn solos in his pieces for orchestra, his operas, and in his two horn concertos. When we think of the sound of a Strauss orchestra, the horns are the center of the focus, just as they often are in Strauss' German predecessor and musical inspiration, Richard Wagner. "Dedication" ("Zueignung") is a song of love and gratitude to a lover or even to a mentor, and it's soaring melody line and stirring accompaniment makes it well suited to the instrument and gratifying and challenging to play.

Scott Joplin: Solace

Scott Joplin (1868-1917) is universally recognized as the most accomplised master of the Ragtime style. Considering this, it's difficult to believe that for most of this century his music languished in obscurity. Joplin's piano pieces were popular during his lifetime, but soon after his death in 1917 his music fell out of the repertory. One can't help but believe that if he had lived just a decade longer, more into the mature recording age, that it would have been a different story. But works of high caliber usually do not go unnoticed forever. The Joplin revival began in the 1970s, and since that time (particularly after the hit movie "The Sting") his music has been played and loved all over the world. "Solace," written in 1909, is one of Joplin's most elegant rags for piano.

Felix Mendelssohn: Then Shall the Righteous Shine Forth from *Elijah*

German composer Felix Mendelssohn (1809-1947) was a brilliant prodigy as a child, and became the most prominent German musician of his day. A great deal of his music continues to be performed regularly today, including his symphonies and concertos, his piano and organ music, music for voice, his chamber pieces, choral music, and his familiar old warhorse, "Wedding March." The oratorio *Elijah* holds a special place in the composer's output. It was premiered not in Germany, but in Birmingham, England, in 1846. It is the story of the fiery prophet of the old testament. Near the end of the oratorio, this noble tenor aria is sung about the rewards of heaven that await the righteous. (Pronunciation tip: Mendelssohn=MEN-del-sun)

Giacomo Carissimi: Victory (Vittoria, mio core)

Carissimi (1605-1674) had a career as a church musician in Rome, and later in life became a priest. He wrote music for chorus and solo voice. Most often these would have been accompanied by some sort of small instrumental ensemble. In the words of the song, the "victory" is in celebrating the heart's healing and getting on with life after being rejected by a lover. (Pronunciation tip: Carissimi=kah-REE-see-mee)

Gabriel Fauré: Fleur jetée

The title can be translated roughly as "discarded flower," but funny as it sounds, "thrown flower" would be more accurate. It's a song of passion and fury. A flower was received from a lover. A betrayal soon followed, and the flower, once a token of affection, is thrown away, saying "let the wind that withers you also wither my heart." Fauré (1845-1924) was one of France's major nineteenth century composers, turning out operas, piano music, orchestra music, chamber works, and choral pieces (the Requiem is well known). But more than any other composer in French history, Fauré excelled in setting poetry to music for the voice to sing, and his many, many songs are at the center of the international repertory of art songs. Fauré became the most important music professor in France, revered for decades at the Paris Conservatoire as the teacher of every French musician of worth. (Pronunciation tips: Fauré=four-AY, Fleur jetèe=fluhr jet-TAY)

BITTERNESS
(Ich grolle nicht)

Nicht zu schnell
(Moderato)

Robert Schumann

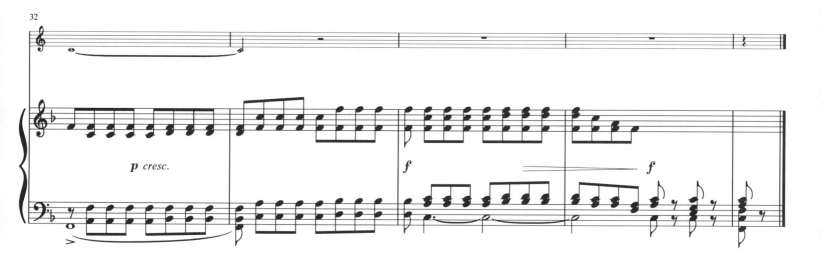

LOVER'S LAMENT
(Una furtiva lagrima)
from THE ELIXIR OF LOVE

Gaetano Donizetti

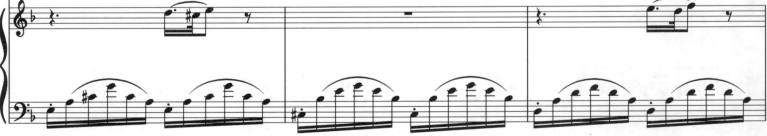

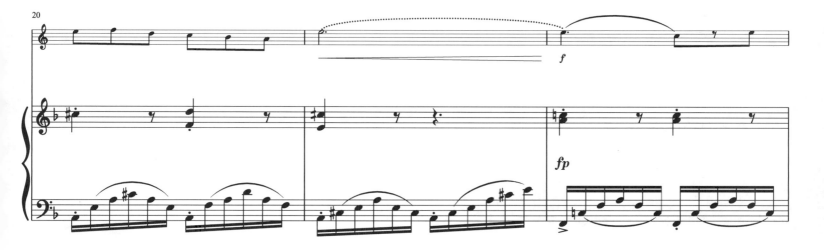

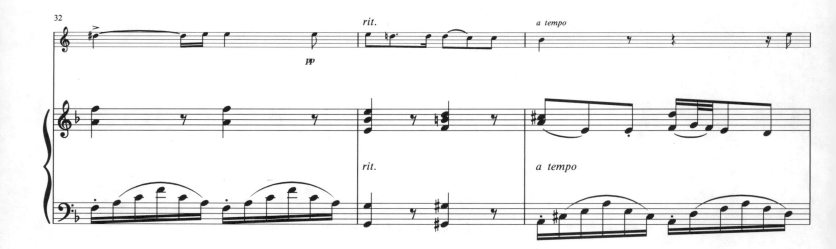

THE GARDENER
(Der Gärtner)

Hugo Wolf

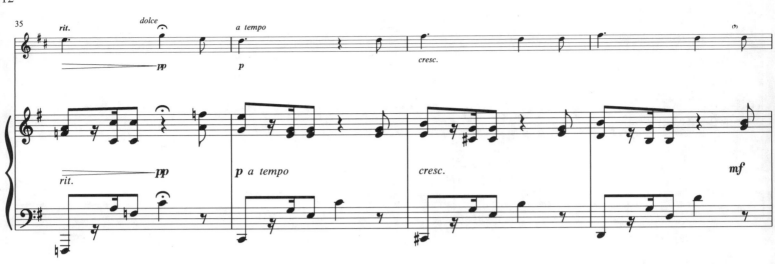

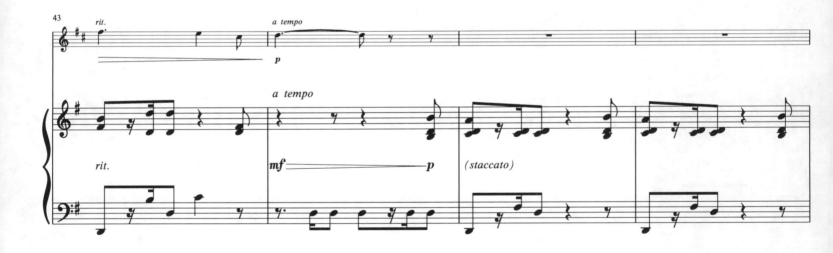

BE THOU WITH ME

(Bist du bei mir)

Johann Sebastian Bach

WELCOME JOY! ADIEU TO SADNESS

from THE SORCERER

Words by W.S. Gilbert
Music by Arthur Sullivan

CHERUBINO'S ARIA

(Non so più cosa son)

from THE MARRIAGE OF FIGARO

Wolfgang Amadeus Mozart

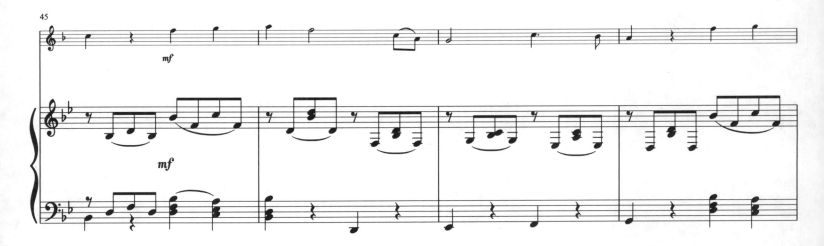

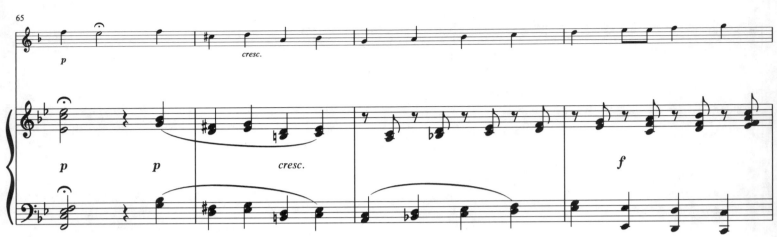

SERENADE
(M'appari tutt' amor)
from MARTHA

Friedrich von Flotow

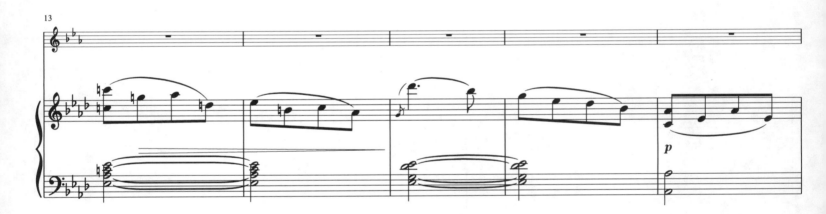

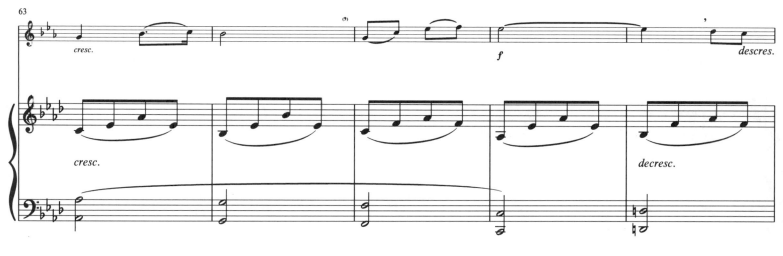

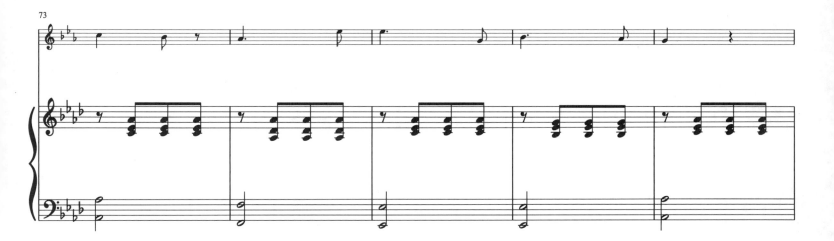

DEDICATION
(Zueignung)

Richard Strauss

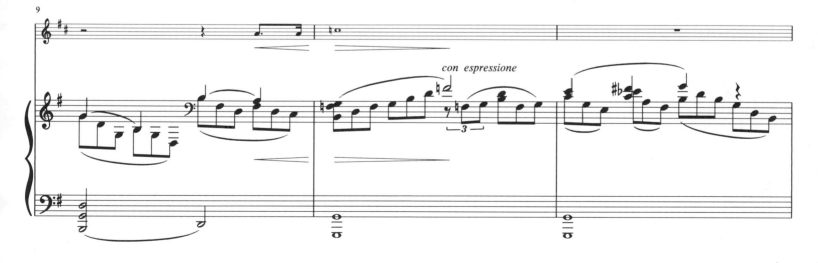

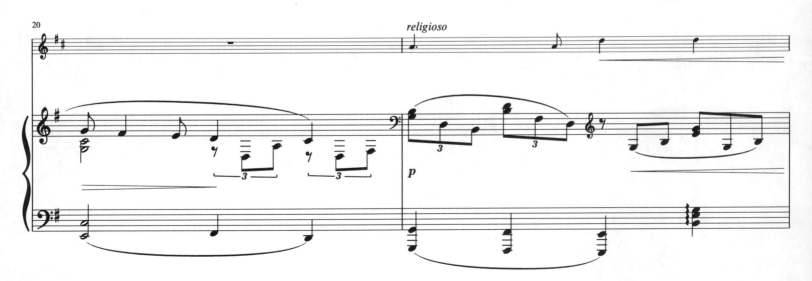

SOLACE

Scott Joplin
Arranged by Rick Walters

Repeats are optional throughout.

THEN SHALL THE RIGHTEOUS SHINE FORTH

from ELIJAH

Felix Mendelssohn

VICTORY
(Vittoria, mio core)

Giacomo Carissimi

Allegro con brio

Horn

Piano

FLEUR JETÉE
(Discarded Flower)

Gabriel Faure

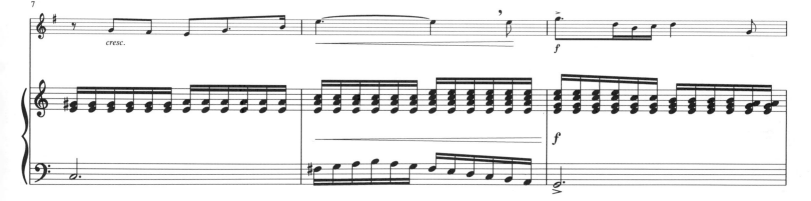

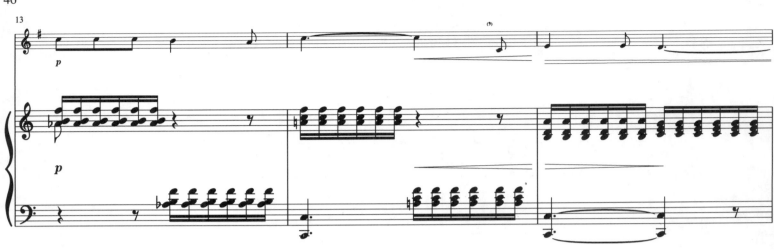

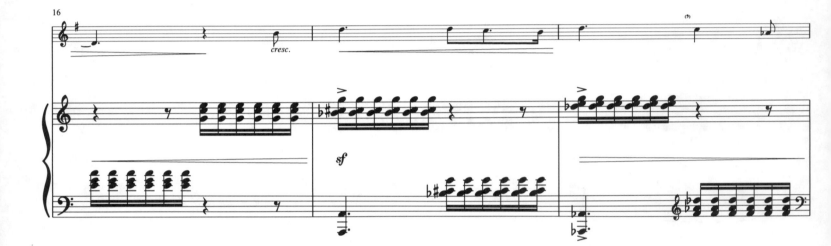

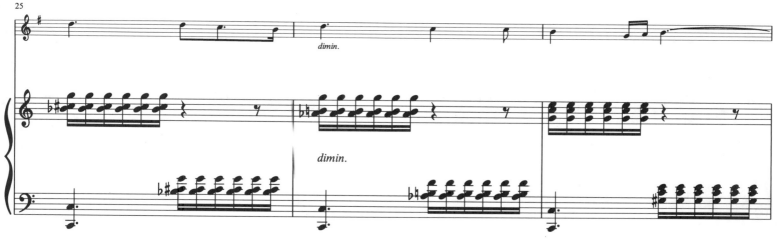

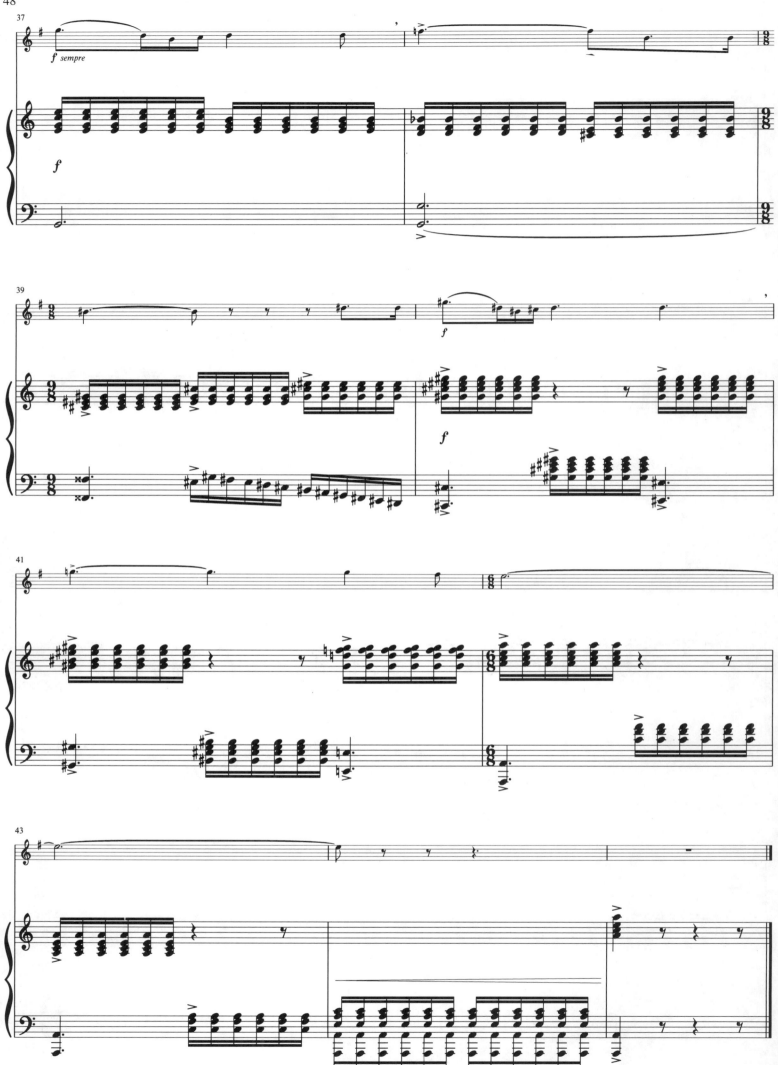